Busy Machines
Trucks

Written by **Amy Johnson**   Illustrated by **Craig Shuttlewood**

MILES KELLY

Out and about

The roads are busy with travelling trucks, big and small, carrying all kinds of loads.

Flatbed truck

They THUNDER...

and TRUNDLE...

Pick-up truck

Van

Lorry

and GROWL!

Dumper truck

Tremendous transporters

Rumbling along, these tough trucks haul heavy cargo.

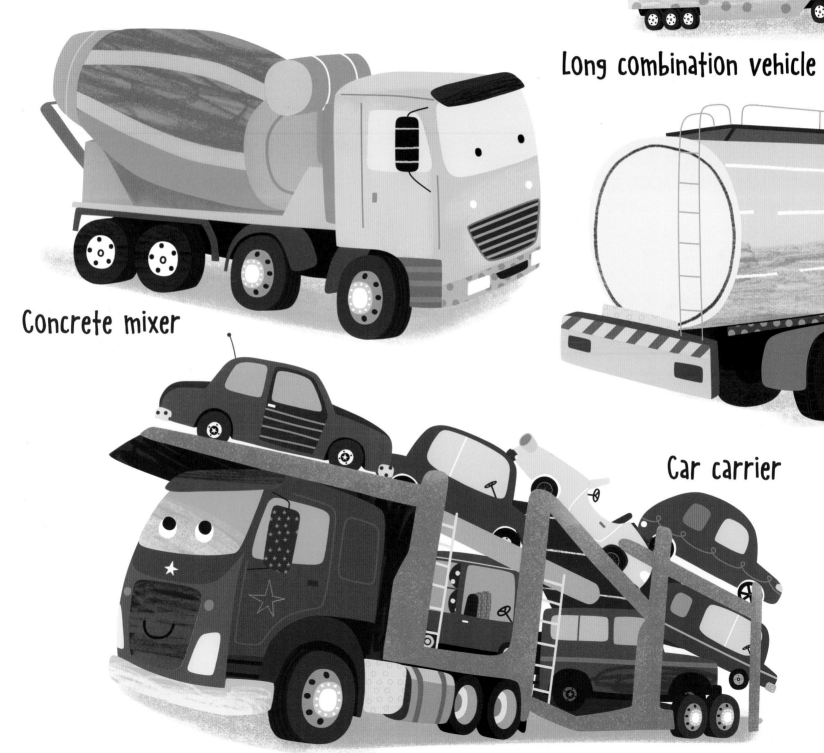

Long combination vehicle

Concrete mixer

Car carrier

Fuel tanker

Container truck

Low loader

Clearing the streets

Street sweepers have speedy spinning brushes that scrub away dirt and rubbish.

Spinning brush →

WHOOSH!

When heavy snow hits, **snow ploughs** work to clear the way.

In cold weather, gritting lorries spread salt on the roads to stop them icing over.

Recycling trucks collect the things you put in your recycling bin.

Monster mayhem

Brightly painted trucks jump and spin, landing on giant tyres – welcome to the monster truck show!

In races, two trucks take on tracks with sharp bends and big jumps

Shock absorbers keep the truck body steady

The trucks do stunts like wheelies and backflips

The body is a big car
or pick-up truck

Massive
off-road tyres

All about lorries

Lorries are big vehicles that carry cargo over long distances. There's lots to be done before the lorry sets out.

This lorry has soft sides that can be opened like a curtain

A forklift truck loads the cargo

Cargo is kept inside the trailer

The trailer is attached to a tractor unit

The driver sits in the cab

There is space inside the cab for drivers to rest and eat — they need to take breaks so they don't get too tired.

Powerful engine

Busy machines!

Delivery time

These hard-working trucks are always on the go. They have plenty of deliveries to make!

The **post van** has lots of parcels and letters to be delivered.

Cargo area works like a giant fridge

Refrigerated trucks keep things cold, so they transport food and drink such as fruit and milk.

A removal van can be stacked high with furniture.

Milk floats aren't used as much today, but you might have seen one!

Delivery trucks deliver parcels that people have ordered online.

Massive movers

High up in the mountains in Chile, two amazing trucks do a special job — they transport huge telescope antennas.

Each antenna weighs 100 tonnes! Moving it takes very powerful engines

Each transporter truck is 20 metres long — that's about the length of five small cars

This transporter is called Lore. Its twin is named Otto

Lore

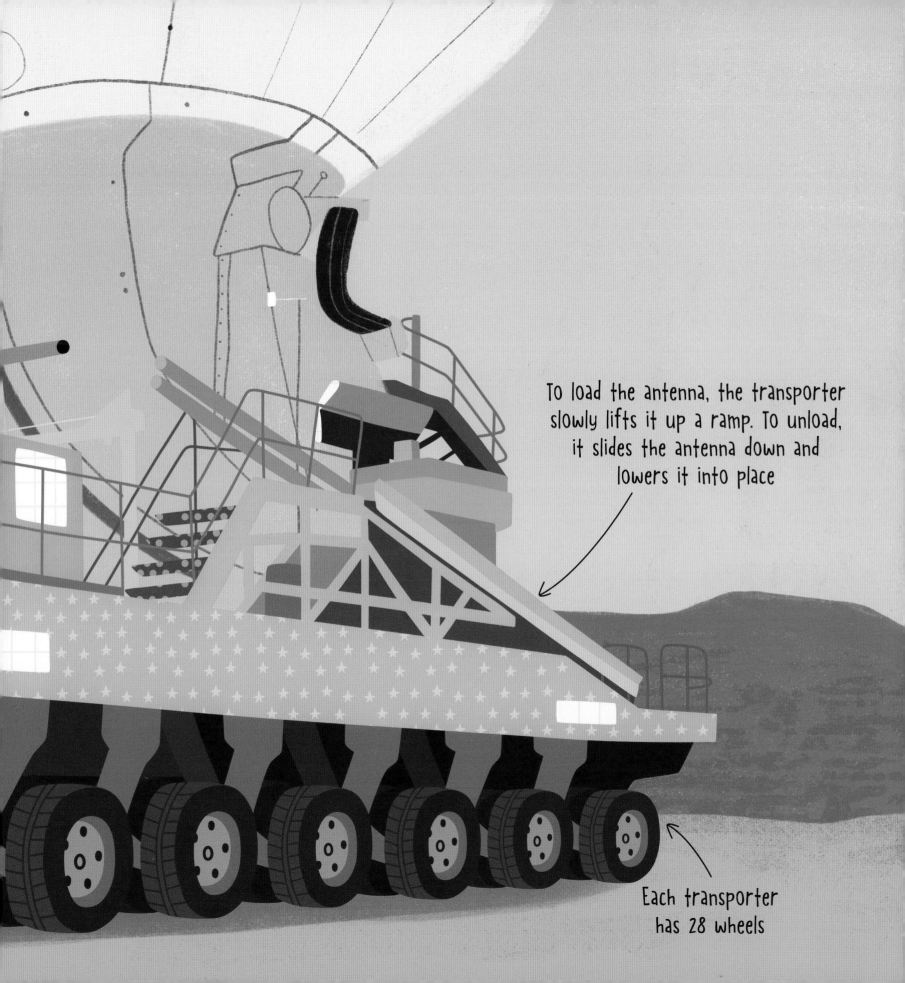

To load the antenna, the transporter slowly lifts it up a ramp. To unload, it slides the antenna down and lowers it into place

Each transporter has 28 wheels

Hard at work

Some trucks are built to take on the toughest jobs, from hauling rocks to fighting fires.

All-terrain truck

Logging truck

Military truck

Fire engine

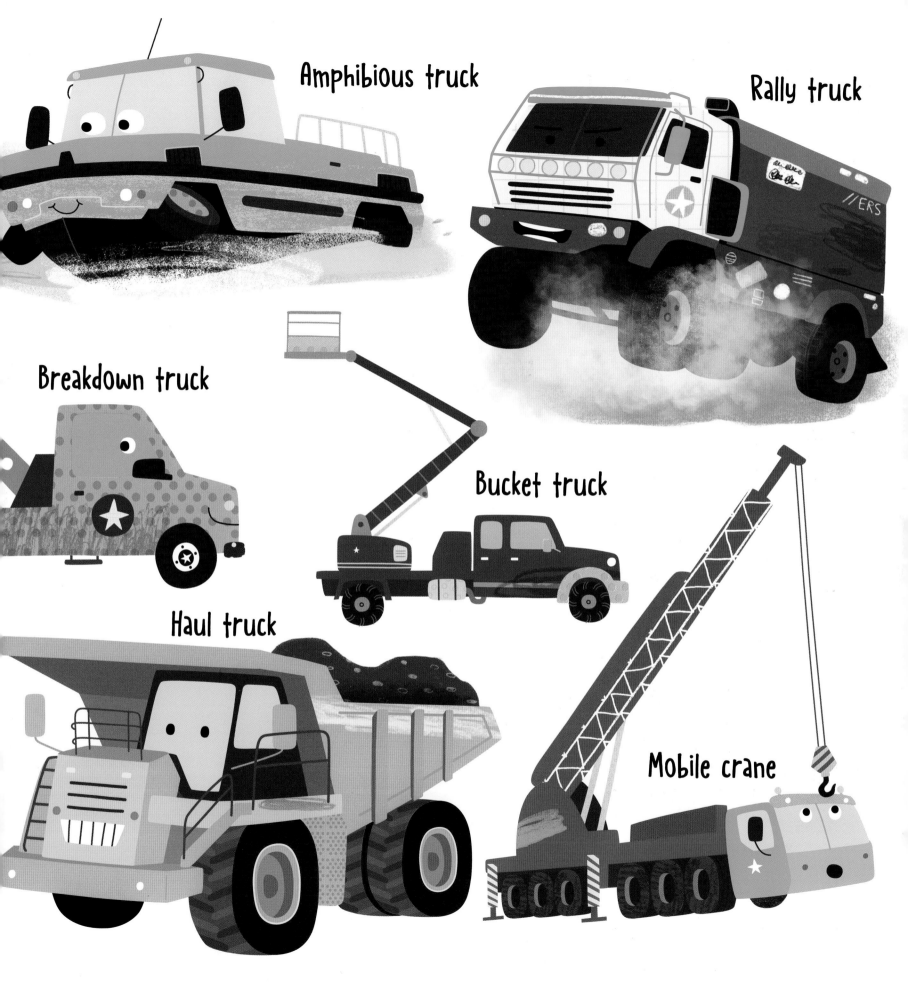

Amphibious truck

Rally truck

Breakdown truck

Bucket truck

Haul truck

Mobile crane

All about car carriers

With shiny new cars packed onto its decks, the towering **car carrier** is ready to go!

Some car carriers have room for 12 cars at once!

The carrier has ramps that can be lifted and tilted to fit the cars on

To keep them safely in place, the cars are tied down by chains or straps

Car carriers usually have two decks. The top deck is filled up first then raised.

Turnaround trucks

A plane has just landed – no time to lose! A team of hard-working trucks get it ready for the next flight.

A **de-icing truck** sprays a special mixture to melt any ice. Its arm can reach the top of the plane.

05

When it's time to go, a **pushback tug** lifts the plane's nose and pushes it away from the gate.

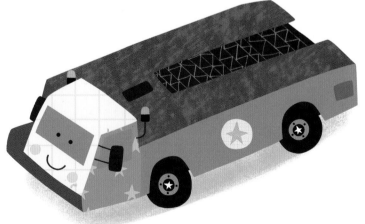

Mobile stairs are driven to the plane for the passengers to board.

Fuel is pumped into the plane by a **refueler**.

Luggage is driven to the plane on a **baggage truck**. It then goes up to the cargo hold on a **belt loader**.

Truck race!

It's time for the trucks to take to the track! They battle it out to be first to the finish.

We speed around the circuit, weaving past each other.

Races are usually 8 to 12 laps. The trucks zip round at up to 160 kilometres per hour